Berry Best Gardening Book

By Megan E. Bryant • Illustrated by SI Artists

Strawberry Shortcake™ © 2004 by Those Characters From Cleveland, Inc. Used under license by Penguin Young Readers Group.
All rights reserved. Published by Grosset & Dunlap, a division of Penguin Young Readers Group,
345 Hudson Street, New York, New York 10014. GROSSET & DUNLAP is a trademark of Penguin Group (USA) Inc. Printed in the U.S.A.

Library of Congress Cataloging-in-Publication Data

Bryant, Megan E.
Berry best gardening book / by Megan E. Bryant ; illustrated by SI Artists.
p.   cm.
"Strawberry Shortcake."
Includes index.
1. Gardening—Juvenile literature.   1. Gardening.   I. S.I. Artists (Group)   II. Title.
SB457.B725 2004 635.9—dc22
2003024469

ISBN 0-448-43552-7

1 3 5 7 9 10 8 6 4 2

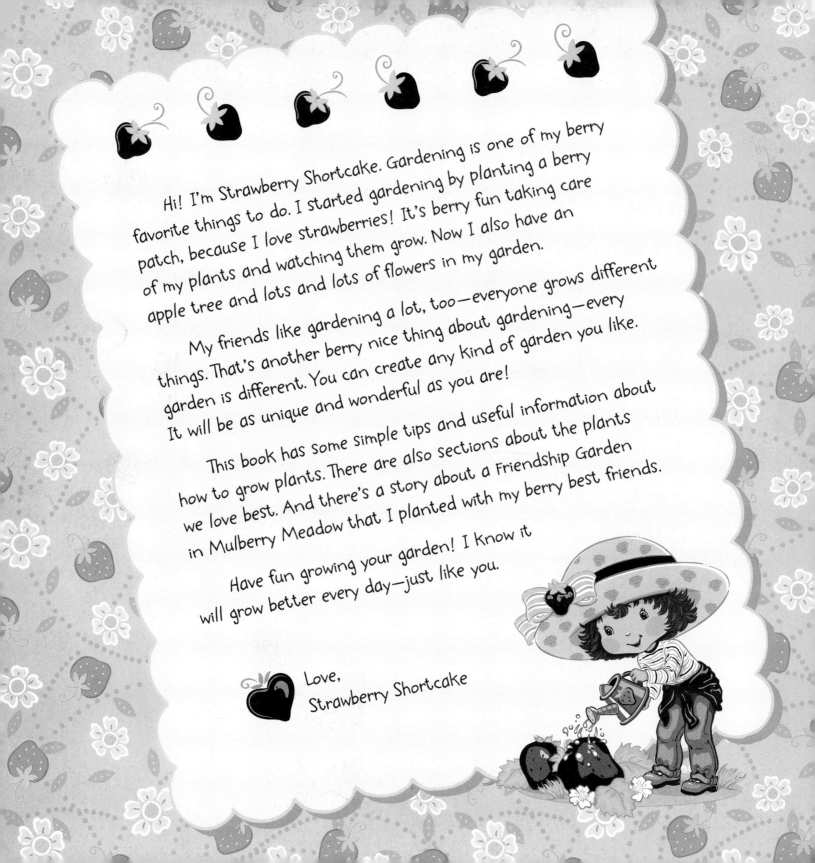

Hi! I'm Strawberry Shortcake. Gardening is one of my berry favorite things to do. I started gardening by planting a berry patch, because I love strawberries! It's berry fun taking care of my plants and watching them grow. Now I also have an apple tree and lots and lots of flowers in my garden.

My friends like gardening a lot, too—everyone grows different things. That's another berry nice thing about gardening—every garden is different. You can create any kind of garden you like. It will be as unique and wonderful as you are!

This book has some simple tips and useful information about how to grow plants. There are also sections about the plants we love best. And there's a story about a Friendship Garden in Mulberry Meadow that I planted with my berry best friends.

Have fun growing your garden! I know it will grow better every day—just like you.

Love,
Strawberry Shortcake

What's Growing On?	4
Gardening Tools	8
Planning and Planting	11
Outdoor Gardens	12
Indoor Gardens	16
Bugs!	20
Your Berry Own Berry Patch	21
Beautiful Bulbs	31
Flower Power	37
Butterfly Gardens	49
Birthday Trees	57
Index	62

What's Growing On?

How do tiny seeds turn into beautiful flowers,
tall trees, and delicious berries?

Plants grow from <u>seeds</u>. First, you have to plant the seed in the soil. Then, add water and let the sun shine in! A tiny <u>root</u> will begin to sprout from the seed. The root stretches down into the soil, where it gets vitamins to feed the plant and make it grow healthy and strong. This part happens underground—since you can't see what's happening, it's like a mystery secretly unfolding in the soil.

STRAWBERRY SHORTCAKE AND THE FRIENDSHIP GARDEN

On a berry pretty day last summer, my friends and I walked down the Berry Trail together, looking for the perfect picnic spot. "Just a little farther, everybody!" Ginger Snap called out. "There's a pretty pasture up ahead."

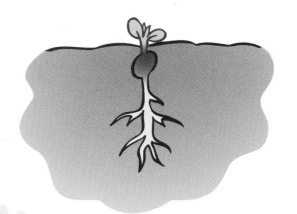

At the same time as the root forms, a tiny <u>shoot</u> also begins to grow out of the seed. But unlike the root, the shoot stretches up, up, up, until it breaks through the soil. Now the fun begins!

As the shoot grows, it becomes a <u>stem</u> and grows leaves (and sometimes flowers, too!).

"Be right there!" I called back. My little sister, Apple Dumplin', was looking at some wildflowers growing by the side of the path. "Come on, Apple, let's hurry!"
Suddenly, Apple Dumplin' tripped and fell over a tangled root!

Plants are living things, and there are two berry important things they need: sunlight and water. Plants turn sunlight into food, and they need water to carry the food through their stems, leaves, and flowers. Water also helps them get nutrients out of the soil. Always make sure the plants in your garden get enough sunlight and water.

"Whoopsie daisy!" I said as I picked Apple Dumplin' up. "Are you okay, sweetheart?"

Apple started giggling as I brushed some dirt off her dress. "Yup!" she said with a smile. "Apple fall down!"

Then I noticed a winding path that I hadn't seen before. It was covered with thick bushes. "I wonder where that path goes," I said. "Wait up, everybody!"

continued on page 8

The <u>flower</u> is where new seeds are formed. On some plants, the flowers turn into fruit or vegetables!

The <u>bud</u> is a baby flower.

The <u>stem</u> holds the plant upright and connects the rest of the plant to the roots.

The <u>leaves</u> turn sunlight into food for the plant.

The <u>roots</u> spread through the soil to get nutrients for the plant.

Gardening Tools

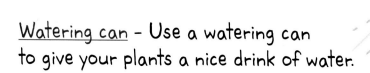

Spade - A spade is like a shovel. It's good for digging large areas and breaking up clumps of dirt.

Trowel - A trowel is a small shovel with a short handle that can be used on smaller areas.

Watering can - Use a watering can to give your plants a nice drink of water.

Spray bottle - A spray bottle can be used to water small, delicate plants, like seedlings, with a gentle mist.

Hose - A hose helps you water large areas in your garden.

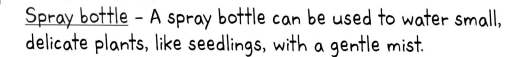

Markers - After you plant your seeds, place markers in the ground next to them to help you remember what you planted where.

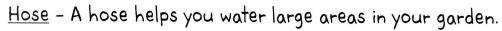

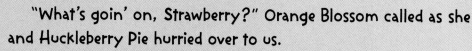

"What's goin' on, Strawberry?" Orange Blossom called as she and Huckleberry Pie hurried over to us.

"I think Apple found a new path," I told them.

"A new path! Let's go!" Huckleberry Pie said excitedly. "Maybe we'll find an adventure down it!"

Fork - This kind of fork isn't for eating your dinner—it's for breaking up clumps of dirt and pulling up weeds and roots!

Hoe - A hoe makes it easier to break up clumps of dirt and to smooth over dug-up soil.

Rake - A rake is good for smoothing out large areas of dirt.

Cutting tools (also called shears or pruners) - Only adults should use these sharp tools. They are helpful for cutting flowers and trimming branches.

Gloves - Wearing gardening gloves will keep your hands from getting scratched (and will keep them from getting dirty, too).

Hat - Always wear a hat when you garden—it will keep the sun out of your eyes and off your face.

Wheelbarrow - Use a wheelbarrow to cart plants and supplies around the garden.

"I don't know," Blueberry Muffin said, looking worried. "We don't know where it goes. What if it's scary?"

"If we stick together and follow Huck's map, we'll be okay!" Angel Cake said, smiling. She reached out for Blueberry's hand.

"Yippee! Let's go!" Ginger Snap yelled, leading the way.

<u>Pots</u> - When you grow plants in pots, you can have them in your yard, on your porch, or in your house—and you can move them around, too.

<u>Plant supports and ties</u> - These can be used to support heavy plants and keep them from falling over.

<u>Plant food</u> - Ask a grown-up to buy plant food at a nursery (a special store that sells lots of things for gardens)—a little extra plant food can help your plants grow big and strong. Only grown-ups should handle plant food, though.

<u>Compost</u> - Compost is a plant's favorite food—and it's easy to make! Save fruit and vegetable scraps, eggshells, coffee grounds, and fallen leaves. Put them in a container in a sunny spot and stir them around once a week. As they rot, they will turn into a rich, healthy soil full of vitamins. Your plants will love it!

The path was covered with overgrown bushes and brambles. There were so many trees overhead that it was awfully dark. But at the end of the path was a berry wonderful surprise—a hidden meadow!

continued on page 12

Planning and Planting

Before you begin your garden, it's always a good idea to plan it out first. Will your garden grow inside or outside? Do you want to grow plants from seeds, or start your garden with young plants? Do you want to grow flowers, fruits, or vegetables—or all three? Thinking about these questions can help you plan and plant a better garden.

OUTDOOR GARDENS

First, decide which plants you want to grow—and how you want to grow them. You can grow plants from seeds, or you can buy baby plants from a nursery, plant them in your yard, and take care of them as they grow.

The meadow was old and overgrown—it looked like no one had been there in a berry long time. It was so full of weeds and fallen leaves that other plants could barely grow.

Blueberry bushes

Raspberry plants

Blueberry bushes

Strawberry plants

Sunflowers

Tulips / Daffodils / Hyacinths

Forget-me-nots / Crocuses

Path

Lilies of the valley

Johnny-jump-ups / Snapdragons

Moonflowers

Morning Glories / Four-o'clocks

Impatiens

Impatiens

Look around your yard to find the best spot for your plants. Different plants need different amounts of light, so make sure you plant them in an area where they will be happy. Some people like to plant tall plants in the back, medium-sized plants in the middle, and short plants in the front. You can plan your garden on a piece of graph paper to make sure the plants are where you want them.

"I wonder where we are," Blueberry Muffin said as she looked around. Huck pulled out his map. "I know!" he said. "Look—this must be Mulberry Meadow. It's right in the middle of our houses!"

Now you can start planting! Using a spade or trowel, dig up the soil in your plot. If you're growing plants from seeds, you need to dig small holes in the soil (follow the directions on the seed package for how deep to dig the holes and how far apart they should be). Drop one seed in each hole, then cover it lightly with soil. When you're done planting the seeds, give them a good drink of water! Add some plant food or compost to get your plants off to a strong start.

That gave me an idea. "Hey, everybody! Let's plant a Friendship Garden here in the meadow! We can work together to make it the berry best garden ever!"

If you're planting baby plants from a nursery, you will need to dig larger holes farther apart. The plants should have a tag stuck into their pots that tells you what to do, but if they don't, you can ask someone at the store. Water the plants until the soil is soaked.

Every few days, check the soil to see if your plants need to be watered—if the soil is damp and moist, you don't need to water, but if it feels dry, give the plant a little drink. When it's hot outside, you may need to water your plants every day. The best time to water is early in the morning or late in the afternoon, when the sun is not so hot. Don't over-water them, though, because giving plants too much water is as bad for them as not having enough.

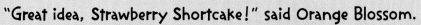

"Great idea, Strawberry Shortcake!" said Orange Blossom.
"Let's plant pretty flowers," Angel Cake said.
"And trees for climbing," said Huck.
"And lots and lots of berries!" Blueberry Muffin added.

INDOOR GARDENS

Growing plants indoors is just as fun as growing an outdoor garden—and it's a little easier, too.

The first thing you need is a container in which to grow your plants. You can buy pots at a garden supply store. They come in all different sizes. You can also grow plants in almost any container you have! Clean, empty milk cartons, yogurt containers, egg cartons, sand buckets, old pie plates, even take-out containers—as long as it will hold soil and water, you can grow a plant in it.

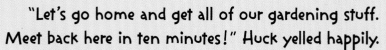

"Let's go home and get all of our gardening stuff. Meet back here in ten minutes!" Huck yelled happily.

Apple Dumplin' and I hurried home as fast as we could. We filled our wheelbarrow with our gardening tools— a rake, a hoe, a spade, and a fork.

Put some pebbles in the bottom of the pot or container—this helps extra water drain out of the pot and keeps dirt from falling out of the tiny hole in the base. Fill the container with dirt, and sprinkle seeds evenly over the top. Next, add a thin layer of dirt on top of the seeds. Place the pot in a sunny location, like on a windowsill, and mist it with a spray bottle so it gets a gentle shower of water.

"Okay, I think we've got everything, Apple," I said. "Let's hurry back to the meadow!"

"Snack?" Apple asked, pointing at some fruit in the kitchen.

"Good idea, Apple! Everybody will want a snack after working in the garden!" We packed up some fresh apples, oranges, and plums to share with our friends.

When the seedlings reach two inches high, you will need to cut some down. If they all try to grow in the same pot, the pot will be too crowded and none of them will grow well. By cutting the weaker seedlings, the stronger ones will have a better chance of growing.

Huckleberry Pie, Ginger Snap, Orange Blossom, Angel Cake, and Blueberry Muffin were all waiting at the meadow by the time we got back.

"Wow," Huck said as he looked around. "There's an awful lot of work to do. Where do we start?"

"Don't worry, Huck, the work will go berry fast if we work together!" I said. "And guess what? Apple and I brought some yummy snacks to share when we finish."

Now have fun taking care of your plant! When it grows too big for its pot, you will need to transplant, or re-pot, it. Fill a larger pot with soil, leaving a big hole for the plant. Then, holding one hand around the plant, slowly turn the pot over so the plant gently falls into your hand. Carefully put it in the larger pot and add soil around it. Then, give your plant a nice drink of water and some plant food so it feels happy in its new home!

"Thanks, Strawberry!" said Ginger Snap. "Now let's get to work!"

Everyone helped pull out the weeds and rake all the fallen leaves. We put them into a bin to make our own compost. We used hoes, rakes, and shovels to dig up the dirt. And before we knew it, our garden was ready to plant!

continued on page 22

19

Bugs!

Bugs are as much a part of the garden as plants are.
Bad bugs eat your plants, but good bugs eat bad bugs—
and help your plants to grow, too!

GOOD BUGS

Bumblebees

Dragonflies

Ladybugs

Roly-poly bugs

Spiders

Worms

BAD BUGS

Aphids

Earwigs

Mealybugs

Slugs and snails

Spider mites

Unless the bad bugs are eating your plants so much that they aren't growing, it's best to let the good bugs fight the bad bugs for you. But if the bad bugs are causing too much damage, try spraying the plant leaves with icy water. You can also sprinkle black pepper around the base of your plants to keep the bad bugs away.

Your Berry Own Berry Patch

I *love* berries—and there's nothing like going into your garden, picking some fresh berries that are warm from the sun, and eating them! Berries aren't always easy to grow, though. They need lots of tender, loving care. If your first berry patch doesn't do very well, don't give up! Keep trying, and one day you'll have a whole crop of big, sweet berries to enjoy.

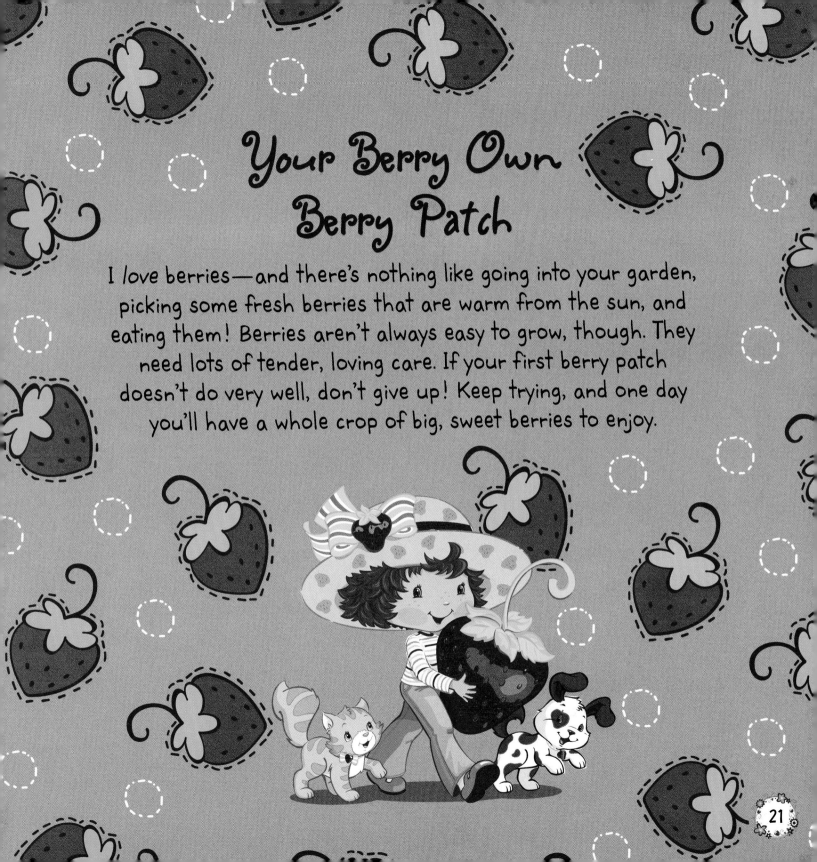

STRAWBERRIES

Strawberries are my berry favorite berries! Their dark green leaves, tiny white flowers, and beautiful red berries make them as nice to look at as they are to eat.

Strawberry plants can be tricky to grow from seeds. Every seed is different, so you never know *what* you might get— a big plant with no berries, a little plant with lots of berries, extra-sweet berries, or not-so-sweet berries. It's fun to grow strawberry plants from seeds to see what will happen, but if you want a big crop of beautiful berries, you should buy baby strawberry plants from a nursery. Pick plants that have same-sized leaves and no flowers.

The first thing we planted was our berry patch, since berries can take a while to grow. Apple Dumplin' and I brought a whole wagon full of baby strawberry plants from our strawberry patch at home. The little green plants were so tiny that they didn't even have any flowers yet!

You can grow strawberry plants in the ground or in a container. If you grow them in the ground, pick a sheltered spot that gets warm sun. Dig holes that are eighteen inches apart (one for each plant). Put each plant in its own hole, then add a layer of compost to fill in the hole and protect the roots. Water the strawberry plants every other day. You can give them compost or liquid plant food once a week.

"I don't see any strawberries," Huckleberry Pie said. He looked berry confused!

"That's because they haven't grown yet," I explained. "These berry plants are still babies. But with some sunshine, some water, and some love, they will grow berry, berry big!"

Soon, you will notice tiny white flowers growing on your strawberry plants. They're berry pretty, but don't pick them—they're the start of the strawberries. Once the flowers begin to turn into berries, put a layer of clean straw between the strawberries and the ground. This keeps the berries berry fresh!

When the strawberries are bright red and sweet-smelling, they are ready to eat! Pick them by the stem (not by the berry), rinse them, and enjoy!

We worked in teams to plant our strawberry plants. Orange Blossom and Angel Cake used hoes to dig up the soil, while Blueberry Muffin and Ginger Snap used their trowels to dig holes for the berry plants.

Then, Huck and I carefully put each plant into its own little hole. Apple Dumplin' helped by watering them!

RASPBERRIES

Raspberries are also berry delicious! Raspberry plants are called <u>canes</u> because they grow upwards on tall stalks. You'll need to grow them near a fence so they can be tied to it, or you can buy or build a special type of fence called a <u>trellis</u> to help them stand up.

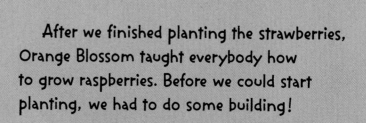

After we finished planting the strawberries, Orange Blossom taught everybody how to grow raspberries. Before we could start planting, we had to do some building!

Buy young raspberry canes from a nursery, then plant them two feet apart, about three inches deep. As the raspberry canes grow taller, tie them to the fence or trellis to help them stay upright.

Raspberries like lots of sun and lots of water. When the raspberry plants begin to flower, you'll know the berries will grow soon. The raspberries are ready to pick when they are deep red, sweet-smelling, and soft (but not too soft!).

Ginger Snap brought her toolbox to the garden, and she showed Huckleberry Pie and Blueberry Muffin how to build trellises. After we planted the raspberry canes, we tied them to the trellises with pretty ribbons in every color!

BLUEBERRIES

My friend Blueberry Muffin taught me all about growing blueberries. You have to be berry patient if you want to grow blueberries from seeds—it takes at least two or three years before you'll have any fruit. If you don't want to wait that long, you can buy two- or three-year-plants from a nursery, and plant them in your garden.

Blueberries grow on bushes that like sunshine, though a little shade during the day is fine, too. Plant them four inches deep and make sure their roots are covered. Because the roots are close to the surface, you'll need to water them every week.

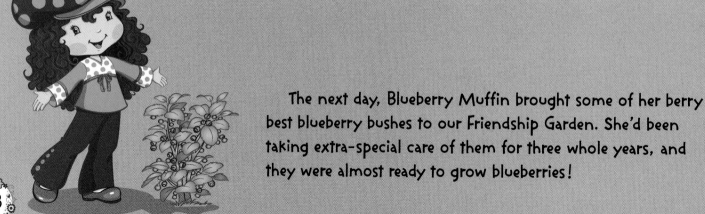

The next day, Blueberry Muffin brought some of her berry best blueberry bushes to our Friendship Garden. She'd been taking extra-special care of them for three whole years, and they were almost ready to grow blueberries!

White flowers on the bush will mean that the berries are on their way—but it will still take several more weeks for the blueberries to grow sweet and turn a pretty shade of bluish-purple. The blueberries are ripe when they fall right off into your hand when touched. Then wash, eat, and enjoy!

Angel Cake and I helped Blueberry Muffin dig some deep holes for the bushes, since they had lots of roots that needed to be covered up. Just after we finished planting them, a rainstorm started. So we didn't need to water them ourselves!

continued on page 32

Berry Tips

People aren't the only ones who love berries. Rabbits, birds, and squirrels also think that berries are a tasty treat. It's berry nice to share your berry patch with wild animals, but if they start eating *all* of your berries, cover the plants with a large net to keep out the critters.

You don't need a big backyard to grow strawberries or blueberries—they can be grown in containers on a porch or deck:

STRAWBERRIES can be grown in a barrel or a special strawberry pot that has little peek-a-boo windows in it. Fill the pot with lots of rich soil and compost, then plant a baby strawberry plant in each hole, filling the pot as you go.

A BLUEBERRY BUSH needs a large container, at least twelve inches wide. Fill the pot with soil, and put compost around the bush to make sure the soil doesn't dry out.

Beautiful Bulbs

Some plants don't grow from seeds—they grow from <u>bulbs</u> instead. A bulb is a funny-looking plant pod that has everything inside it that it needs to grow. And the best part is that after you plant the bulb, it can bloom year after year!

Bulbs need to be planted in the fall—they like a nice long, quiet winter to sleep and get ready for growing. It's good to water them right after you plant them, but after that they don't need much water at all. When spring comes, look out! Bulbs pop up with all sorts of pretty flowers as one of the first signs that spring has sprung.

Here are some of my berry favorite bulbs:

DAFFODILS

Daffodils are berry easy to grow! There are over one thousand different kinds of daffodils, but they all come in sunny shades of yellow, orange, and white. There's a simple trick to planting daffodil bulbs—their holes should be twice as deep as the bulbs are long. So if the bulb is two inches long, plant it four inches deep. Daffodils like lots of sun, but they're such happy flowers, they will grow almost anywhere (as long as they aren't in a completely shady spot). Give them a good soaking when you first plant them in the fall, then water them lightly in the spring.

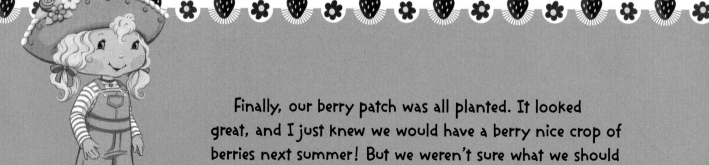

Finally, our berry patch was all planted. It looked great, and I just knew we would have a berry nice crop of berries next summer! But we weren't sure what we should plant next—until Angel Cake had a berry good idea.

CROCUSES

Cute little crocuses are usually the first flowers to bloom in spring. They come in cheery colors of purple, white, and yellow, and only grow about three inches high. They like lots of sun, but need very little water. Plant each bulb two to three inches deep, three to four inches apart. They're so tiny and pretty—plant lots and lots!

"Fall will be here soon," she said. "Then winter, and we won't be able to do much in the garden at all. Let's plant some bulbs, so when spring comes, our garden will be full of flowers right away!"

So that's exactly what we did!

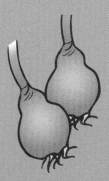

HYACINTHS

This bulb has a hard name to say, but it grows the sweetest-smelling flowers imaginable! Hyacinths come in bright shades of crimson, purple, deep blue, and snowy white. Plant them four inches deep, and water them well. If you have a dry winter, they will need extra water in the spring.

The next time we worked in the garden, everyone brought something for planting bulbs. I brought crocus bulbs, Angel Cake brought lily of the valley bulbs, Ginger Snap brought tulip bulbs, Orange Blossom brought daffodil bulbs, and Blueberry Muffin brought hyacinth bulbs.

TULIPS

Pretty tulips stand tall on their stalks. They come in many shades of red, pink, yellow, purple, and white. Find a sunny spot in your garden and plant the bulbs six to eight inches deep. Don't forget to give them lots of water and compost when you plant them!

LILIES OF THE VALLEY

These tiny flowers look like little white bells—and they smell beautiful. There is even a song about them! Lilies of the valley like to grow in shady areas, getting a bit of sun during the day. Plant the bulbs one inch below the surface of the soil, six inches apart. They'll spread like crazy around your whole yard if you let them!

Huck didn't bring any bulbs, but he brought a special tool called a bulb planter that made it berry easy to plant them.

continued on page 38

Bulb Tips

- Always remember to plant BULBS with the pointy end up!

- Try planting BULBS in clumps so you will have clusters of flowers in the spring.

- Some BULBS are poisonous, so make sure you never put them in your mouth. Keep them away from pets and little brothers and sisters, too.

- After the flowers have finished blooming, don't cut down their leaves—even if they look dried-out and ugly. The leaves may look dead, but they are actually making food for the bulb to live off, until it blooms again next spring!

Flower Power

There are thousands and thousands of different flowers you can grow in your garden—big flowers, little flowers, sweet-smelling flowers, flowers in every color of the rainbow! You can look through a seed catalog to pick the ones you want to grow. These are some of my berry favorites!

Tiny Treats

I always love growing tiny flowers. It's so much fun to find the sweet little blooms hiding in corners of the garden! Take a peek at them under a magnifying glass if you want a better look at their miniature petals and tiny leaves. These little blossoms are just the right size for doll bouquets. I even decorate my dollhouse with them!

SWEET WILLIAMS

Sweet Williams are a type of tiny carnation that grows in clumps. They like lots of sun, but they usually only need to be watered once a week. They grow great in containers, too, and come in almost any color. When you plant the seeds, put just a tiny bit of soil (⅛ inch) on top of them.

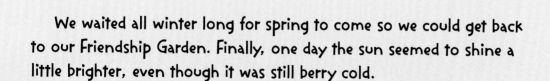

We waited all winter long for spring to come so we could get back to our Friendship Garden. Finally, one day the sun seemed to shine a little brighter, even though it was still berry cold.

JOHNNY-JUMP-UPS

These little pansies spread by themselves and pop up all over the garden, like they are jumping from spot to spot! They come in lots of colors and sometimes have beautiful markings, like purple petals with yellow stripes. Johnny-jump-ups grow best in spring and fall because they like mild weather. Plant them under a thin layer of soil. It's best to take care of your Johnny-jump-ups in the morning—they like morning sun, and you should only water them in the morning, too.

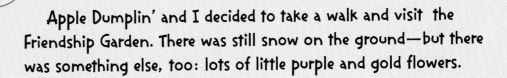

Apple Dumplin' and I decided to take a walk and visit the Friendship Garden. There was still snow on the ground—but there was something else, too: lots of little purple and gold flowers.

FORGET-ME-NOTS

These teeny-tiny flowers grow in pretty shades of blue or pink. Their name is as sweet as their blossoms, and makes these flowers perfect for giving to your friends and family. Plant the seeds five inches apart after winter ends. After they start growing, cut down every other one. They love growing in shady areas and don't need too much water.

Over the next few weeks, the sun grew warmer, the snow melted, and the rest of the bulbs we had planted began to bloom. Soon, it was time to get back to work in the garden.

Flowers by the Hour

These funny flowers only bloom at certain times each day!

MORNING GLORIES

These bright flowers bloom first thing in the morning, and close up around early afternoon. They come in shades from the palest pink to royal purple and crimson. As soon as the weather grows warm, soak the seeds overnight. Then, plant them in a sunny place under ½ inch of soil. If it's dry out, water them every few days to make sure the soil stays moist. Morning glories are climbers—they need a fence or trellis to wrap their vines around. Some morning glories can grow ten feet tall! They only last for a few hours before they close up, but don't worry—a new batch of flowers will bloom every morning.

Everyone helped clean up the dead leaves and plants and added them to the compost. We gave the berry patch some plant food. Then, we planned different sections for planting flowers.

FOUR-O'CLOCKS

These pretty, sweet-smelling flowers grow on bushes. They open in the late afternoon (around four o'clock!) and bloom all night long, until they close the next morning. Plant four-o'clocks in the yard when winter is over, sowing the seeds twelve inches apart. They will start growing in only seven to ten days! Four-o'clocks come in colors like red, yellow, pink, white, or with stripes. They make their own seeds, too, so don't be surprised if they spread around your garden.

One berry rainy day, everybody met up at Angel Cake's house to make some pretty plant markers for our garden. We drew pictures of the plants on construction paper and then covered them with plastic. We even put stickers on them!

"Rain, rain, rain!" Huck complained. "It's been raining every day! We'll never get to plant our garden if it keeps up."

MOONFLOWERS

Moonflowers are large, white flowers that look like a full moon—but they probably got their name because they don't open until dusk. Then they bloom all night long, and make the air smell like perfume! Like morning glories, moonflowers grow on vines, so they need a fence or trellis to climb up. Plant them the same way you plant morning glories. In fact, you can plant moonflowers and morning glories in the same planter and have lovely flowers blooming all day and night!

"Don't worry, Huck," I said. "All this rain will make our garden extra-beautiful! It's getting warmer every day, too, and as soon as the rain stops, we can plant some seeds. I have a feeling we'll be planting our garden berry soon."

"And I can't wait!" Ginger Snap exclaimed.

Flower Fun

SNAPDRAGONS

Snapdragons make fun flower puppets! The blossoms look like little dragon faces, and you can squeeze them to make the "dragons" talk. They come in every color of the rainbow, and can grow berry tall—up to four feet! (The smallest ones are only six inches tall.) Each snapdragon needs lots of space, so don't crowd the seeds—allow at least twelve inches between them. Plant the seeds near the very top of the soil. Snapdragons like lots of sun, though a little shade is okay. Always try to water them close to the roots, instead of pouring water on them from the top. They start off slow, but once they start blooming, you can have a whole puppet show.

Sure enough, a few days later the sky cleared, the sun came out, and it was time to plant the rest of our garden. On a bright Saturday near the end of spring, we had a planting party in our Friendship Garden! Everyone brought a snack to share and paired up to plant the flower seeds.

IMPATIENS

These cheery flowers like growing in shady spots, and can brighten up your garden with their clean white blossoms or shocking pink and electric red ones. But what I like best about impatiens is that they are like little garden firecrackers! Some people call them poppers because as the seeds grow inside the flower, the seed pod swells—it grows bigger and bigger until it can't hold any more seeds. Then, all you have to do is touch it and—*pop!*—it will explode, scattering seeds all around. It's berry fun! So find a shady spot in your garden, sow some impatien seeds near the surface of the soil, and wait for your "poppers" to grow.

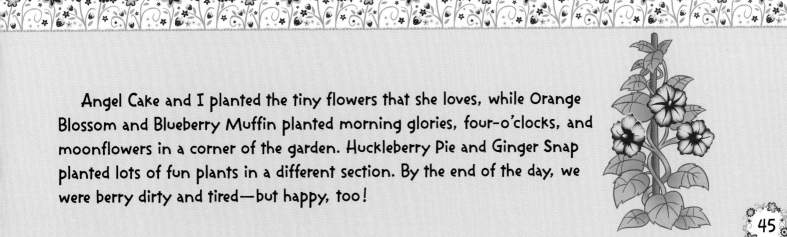

Angel Cake and I planted the tiny flowers that she loves, while Orange Blossom and Blueberry Muffin planted morning glories, four-o'clocks, and moonflowers in a corner of the garden. Huckleberry Pie and Ginger Snap planted lots of fun plants in a different section. By the end of the day, we were berry dirty and tired—but happy, too!

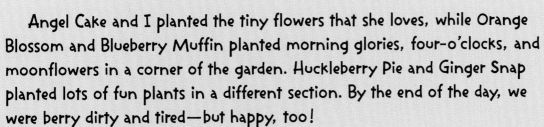

SUNFLOWERS

I love eating sunflower seeds—but I love growing sunflowers even more! You can plant them in your yard or in a large pot. "Dwarf" sunflowers grow only eighteen inches tall, but large sunflowers can grow ten to fifteen feet tall. Plant the seeds under an inch of soil, twelve inches apart. Make sure they get lots of water and lots of sun.

It wasn't long before tiny green shoots started to sprout up. Our flowers were really growing! We took turns watering them—but we were berry careful not to give them *too* much water.

If you want to grow giant sunflowers, plant them near a fence or post that you can tie them to as they grow—this will help protect them from wind or stormy weather. After a few weeks, your sunflowers will start to poke out of the ground. Soon, you will have large golden flowers with dark brown centers—which will turn into seeds by the end of summer! Birds and squirrels will want to eat all the seeds, but try to save some for yourself. Ask an adult to roast them in the oven, sprinkle them with salt, and enjoy! Yum!

Apple Dumplin' and I went to the Friendship Garden almost every day to see how it was growing. And we usually ran into one of our friends there!

continued on page 50

Flower Tips

Flowers need careful watering. It's berry important not to over-water them, but if the weather is dry or hot, give them a nice long soaking. You can buy a little tool at the nursery that changes color when the soil is too dry, or you can make one out of a large stone. Poke half of the stone into the soil; leave the other half sticking out. If the part of the stone in the soil is dry, water the plants. If it is damp, they don't need water.

Many flowers make seeds to grow new plants. Watch your flowers carefully for seedpods. When the seedpods look dry, you can break them open and collect the seeds. Save them in a paper envelope (don't forget to write down what kind of seeds they are) and plant them next year.

It's berry nice to pick some of your flowers and bring them inside to brighten your house. Put them in a vase and give them fresh water every day to help them last longer.

Butterfly Gardens

Butterflies are so pretty as they flutter by! If you want lots of butterflies to visit your garden, plant the flowers on the next few pages. Butterflies love them!

All About Butterflies

To grow a garden for butterflies, it helps to know how butterflies grow! An adult butterfly lays small white eggs on a leaf. When an egg hatches, a caterpillar comes out. The caterpillar eats and eats and eats and eats, until finally, it's not hungry anymore. Then, the caterpillar makes a cocoon around itself. Inside the cocoon, it goes through a big change. You can't see what's happening, but it's turning into a butterfly! Two or three weeks later, an adult butterfly comes out of the cocoon. It stretches its beautiful wings, dries them out in the sun, and then takes off, flying through the sky!

Our garden was growing more and more every day! There were flowers on the berry plants and lots of blooms from the bulbs. The tiny shoots were growing bigger and stronger. But there was still a section of the garden that was empty and bare—until Orange Blossom had an idea.

Butterflies can't eat food the way other bugs can—they can only drink. Their favorite drink is the sweet nectar from deep inside flowers. Butterflies have a long, curly tongue that is like a straw. They stick it into flowers and suck up the nectar. But butterflies can be awfully picky. They prefer nectar that comes from pink, purple, and red flowers that grow in the sun. So if you love butterflies as much as I do, you can make a special corner of your garden just for them by filling it with their favorite foods!

"I love butterflies—and they're berry good for gardens," she told us. "Maybe that corner of our garden could be just for butterflies! We can plant their favorite flowers and make a safe space for them."

BUTTERFLY BUSH

Butterflies love this bush so much that it was named after them! It has long leaves that they can lay their eggs on. After they hatch, caterpillars love to munch the leaves. And butterfly bushes have zillions of tiny, bright purple flowers that are just the right size for butterflies. Butterfly bushes take a berry long time to grow from seeds, so it's best to buy a small bush at the nursery and let it grow up in your yard. Plant it in a sunny spot that is sheltered from wind, and water it when the soil seems dry.

"That's a great idea, Orange Blossom! I love butterflies, too," I told her. We read a book about all the plants that butterflies love best. Then we decided to plant cosmos, lavender, honeysuckle, and a butterfly bush.

COSMOS

Cosmos are berry easy to grow, and their bright flowers and tall stalks can bring butterflies from all around! Plant cosmos seeds in late spring under ⅛ inch of soil. Make sure you know what size you're getting—cosmos range from fourteen inches to five feet tall! Cosmos need less water than other plants, and they will be okay even if the soil is dry.

After we planted a butterfly garden, we built some birdhouses and bird-feeders. Ginger Snap let everybody borrow her tools, and Angel Cake brought her prettiest paints. Soon, we had a whole village of bright birdhouses!

HONEYSUCKLE

Honeysuckle is a shrub that can grow tall vines if there is a fence or trellis for the vines to wrap around. It has delicate little flowers that smell as sweet as honey! Butterflies love the flowers, and birds love the honeysuckle berries (but the berries are **not** good for people). In the summer, give your honeysuckle bush lots of water.

Every day, more and more beautiful butterflies and birds come to our garden! The birds have built nests in the birdhouses and there are little baby birds that live there, too.

LAVENDER

Lavender is an herb that smells wonderful! It has dozens of tiny purple flowers on tall stalks. Dig a deep hole in your butterfly garden to cover the roots of your lavender plant. It doesn't need to be watered often, but make sure you give it a nice long drink when you do water it.

One time, when I was berry still, a butterfly even landed on my nose!

I held my breath while it sat there. Its wings fluttered for a moment and then it flew off.

continued on page 58

Butterfly Garden Tips

Butterflies love to sunbathe. It's berry nice to put some flat, dark stones in your garden—the sun will warm the stones, and the butterflies can rest on them!

Besides nectar, butterflies also need to drink water. You can put a small birdbath in your garden—birds and butterflies will use it! Or, put several small, shallow dishes of water in the garden (add a sprinkle of salt to them to give the butterflies some minerals).

Butterflies are as delicate as they are beautiful. Don't ever use any chemicals or pesticides in your butterfly garden. Let all bugs enjoy the butterfly garden—you'll see that your plants will turn out just fine.

Birthday Trees

Planting a birthday tree is a berry nice birthday present for someone special! Trees are good for the earth, and they give us shelter from wind and storms. When you plant a tree on your birthday, you and the tree get to grow up together. You might start out taller than your birthday tree, but after a few years, the tree will be taller than you!

Here are some ideas for your birthday tree:

- 🍓 A fruit tree, like apple, cherry, plum, or peach
- 🍓 A flowering tree, like dogwood or magnolia
- 🍓 An evergreen tree, like pine, juniper, or holly

Buy a young tree from a nursery, and dig a deep, round hole that will cover all of its roots. If the summer is very dry or hot, water your tree. You can also give it special plant food for trees or compost. Every year, have a birthday party with your tree! Hang a bird-feeder on it so the birds can celebrate, too.

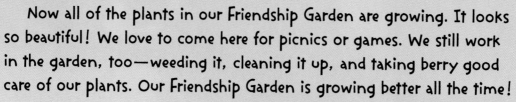

Now all of the plants in our Friendship Garden are growing. It looks so beautiful! We love to come here for picnics or games. We still work in the garden, too—weeding it, cleaning it up, and taking berry good care of our plants. Our Friendship Garden is growing better all the time!

THE END

Spring

Summer

CYCLE
OF
SEASONS

Winter

Fall

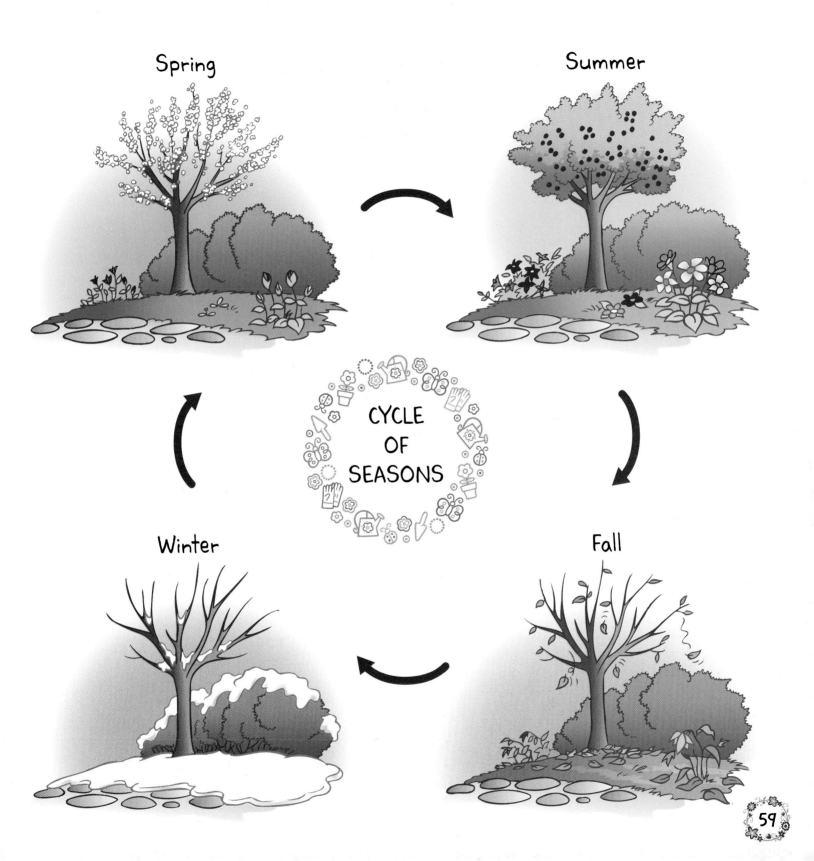

Get Growing!

I hope that this book helps you start your own garden!
Gardens need love and care, but they'll give you sweet berries,
beautiful flowers, and a wonderful place for you to have
picnics, play in, and spend time with your friends and family.
Don't give up if your garden gets off to a slow start—be patient
and take good care of the plants, and someday your garden
will grow just as well as you do!

Index

A

activities
    making compost, 10
    roasting sunflower seeds, 46–47
adults
    buying and handling plant food, 10
    help with cutting tools, 9
afternoon sun
    and four-o'clocks, 42
animals, 30
aphids, 20
apple trees, 58

B

berries
    about, 21, 30
    blueberries, 28–29
    honeysuckle berries, 54
    raspberries, 26–27
    strawberries, 22–25
berry patch, 21
birdbaths, 56
bird-feeders, 58
birds, 30
    and honeysuckle berries, 54
    and sunflower seeds, 46–47
birthday trees, 57–58
blueberries, 28–29
buds, 7
bugs, 20
    getting rid of bad bugs, 20
    in butterfly gardens, 56
bulbs
    about, 31, 36
    crocuses, 33
    daffodils, 32
    hyacinths, 34
    lilies of the valley, 35
    tulips, 35

bumblebees, 20

bushes
    blueberry bushes, 28–29
    butterfly bushes, 52
    and four-o'clocks, 42
butterflies, 49–56
butterfly bush, 52
butterfly gardens, 49–56

C

canes, 26–27
caterpillars, 50–53
cherry trees, 58
cocoon, 50–51
compost
    how to make, 10
    and strawberries, 23–24
    and trees, 58
    and tulips, 34
containers, 16–17
    and blueberries, 30
    and strawberries, 30
cosmos, 53
crocuses, 33
crowding
    in pot, 18–19
    and snapdragons, 44
cutting
    adult help, 9
    forget-me-nots, 40
    seedlings, 18
cutting tools, 9

D

daffodils, 32
digging, 8–9, 10, see also holes
dirt, see soil
dogwood trees, 58
dragonflies, 20

E

earwigs, 20
eating
    how a butterfly eats, 50–51
    strawberries, 22–24

sunflower seeds, 46–47
evergreen trees, 58

F

fall, 31, 59
fence
    and moonflowers, 43
    and morning glories, 41
    and raspberries, 26–27
    and sunflowers, 46–47
flowering trees, 58
flowers
    about, 37, 48
    on blueberry bushes, 29
    cosmos, 53
    crocuses, 33
    daffodils, 32
    diagram of how they grow, 7
    forget-me-nots, 40
    four-o'clocks, 42
    and fruits and vegetables, 7
    honeysuckle, 54
    hyacinths, 34
    impatiens, 45
    Johnny-jump-ups, 39
    lavender, 55
    lilies of the valley, 35
    moonflowers, 43
    morning glories, 41
    and seeds, 7
    snapdragons, 44
    on strawberry plants, 22–25
    sunflowers, 46–47
    Sweet Williams, 38
    tulips, 34

food
    buying plant food, 10
    for plants from compost, 10
    in plants, from water and sunlight, 6
    in seeds for baby plants, 6
forget-me-nots, 40
fork, 9
four-o'clocks, 42
fruit trees, 58

G

garden
    indoor, 16–19
    outdoor, 12–15
    planning, 11

gardening tools, 8–10

gloves, 9

growing
    indoors, 16–19
    outdoors, 12–15
    water and sunlight, 6

H

hat, 9

heavy plants
    support with ties, 10

hoe, 9

holes
    for baby plants, 14–15
    for blueberries, 28
    for crocuses, 33
    for daffodils, 32
    for hyacinths, 34
    for lilies of the valley, 35
    for raspberries, 27
    for seeds, 14
    spacing and depth, 14–15
    for strawberries, 23
    for tulips, 35

holly trees, 58

honeysuckle, 54

hose, 8

hyacinths, 34

I

impatiens, 45

indoor gardens, 16–19

J

Johnny-jump-ups, 39

juniper trees, 58

L

ladybugs, 20

lavender, 55

leaves
    diagram of flower, 7
    on flowers after blooming, 36
    turn sunlight into food, 6

light
    different amounts for different plants, 13

lilies of the valley, 35

M

magnolia trees, 58

markers, 8

mealybugs, 20

moonflowers, 43

morning glories, 41–42

morning sun
    and Johnny-jump-ups, 39
    and morning glories, 41

N

nectar, 51, 56

night
    and four-o'clocks, 42
    and moonflowers, 43

nursery
    about, 10
    buying plant food, 10
    plants from, 15

nutrients
    roots spreading through soil to get
     to plants, 6
    salt, minerals for butterflies, 56
    and water, 6
    see also vitamins

O

outdoor gardens, 12–15

P

paper
    planning a garden on graph paper, 12–13

peach trees, 58

pebbles, 17

pepper, to get rid of bugs, 20

pets, 36

picking
    blueberries, 29
    raspberries, 27
    strawberries, 24–25

pine trees, 58

planning your garden, 11

plant food, see food

planting
    indoors, 16–19
    outdoors, 12–15

plants
    about, 6
    diagram, 7
    growing from seeds, 4–5

plant supports, see ties

plum trees, 58

poisonous
    bulbs, 36
    honeysuckle berries, 54
    pesticides and chemicals, 56

"poppers," 45

pots
    about, 10
    and blueberries, 30
    changing sizes for growing plants, 18–19
    and strawberries, 30

pruners, 9

puppets, 44

R

rabbits, 30

rake, 9

raspberries, 26–27

roly-poly bugs, 20

roots
    of blueberry bush, 28–29
    diagram, 7
    growing from seeds, 4–5

rotting, and compost, 10

S

seedlings, 18

seedpods
    and impatiens, 45
    saving in an envelope, 48

seeds
    diagram, 7
    digging holes for, 14
    food for baby plant, 6
    how they grow, 4–6

sunflower seeds, 46–47
  where formed, 6

shade-loving plants
  forget-me-nots, 40
  impatiens, 45
  lilies of the valley, 35

shears, 9

shoots
  growing from seeds, 4–5

size
  different size plants and where
    to plant, 13

slugs, 20

snails, 20

snapdragons, 44

soil
  covering seeds, 14–15
  and Johnny-jump-ups, 39
  and plants, 4–5
  on Sweet Williams, 38
  and tools, 8–9, 10
  and water; checking soil, 14–15

spacing
  between raspberry plants, 27
  for snapdragons, 44

spade
  about, 8
  planting with, 14–15

spider mites, 20

spiders, 20

spray bottle, 8
  using indoors, 17

spreading flowers
  four-o'clocks, 42
  Johnny-jump-ups, 39
  lilies of the valley, 35

spring, 31, 59

squirrels, 30
  and sunflower seeds, 46–47

stem
  diagram, 7
  growing from shoot, 4–5
  holds plant upright, 7
  picking strawberries by, 24–25

stones
  for butterflies, 56
  to gauge wetness of soil, 48

straw, 24–25

strawberries, 22–25

summer, 59

sun, *see* sunlight; *see also* afternoon sun;
  morning sun

sunlight
  and butterflies, 56
  food for plants, 6
  and leaves, 7
  and plants, 6

sun-loving plants
  blueberries, 28–29
  butterfly bush, 52
  crocuses, 33
  daffodils, 32
  raspberries, 26–27
  snapdragons, 44
  strawberries, 22–25
  sunflowers, 46–47
  Sweet Williams, 38
  tulips, 35

supports, 10

sweet-smelling flowers
  four-o'clocks, 42
  honeysuckle, 54
  hyacinths, 34
  lavender, 55
  lilies of the valley, 35
  moonflowers, 43
  Sweet Williams, 38

T

tall flowers
  cosmos, 53
  morning glories, 41
  snapdragons, 44
  sunflowers, 46–47
  where to plant, 13

ties, 10

tiny flowers
  crocuses, 33
  forget-me-nots, 40
  Johnny-jump-ups, 39
  lilies of the valley, 35
  on strawberries, 24–25
  Sweet Williams, 38

transplant, 19

trees
  birthday trees, 57–59
  evergreen: holly, juniper, pine, 58
  flowering: dogwood, magnolia, 58
  fruit: apple, cherry, plum, peach, 58

trellis
  and honeysuckle, 54
  and moonflowers, 43
  and morning glories, 41
  and raspberries, 26

trowel
  about, 8
  planting with, 14

tulips, 35

V

vitamins
  in compost, 10
  gathered by roots, 4
  from soil, 4–5
  see also nutrients

W

water
  cold, to get rid of bugs, 20
  and sunlight, for plants, 6

watering can, hose, and spray bottle, 8

watering
  best time for, 14–15
  checking if plants need water, 14–15
  hose, 8
  over-watering, 14–15
  spray bottle, 8
  strawberries, 23
  tips, 48
  watering can, 8
  and weather, 15

watering can, 8

wheelbarrow, 9

winter, 59

worms, 20

Strawberry Shortcake™

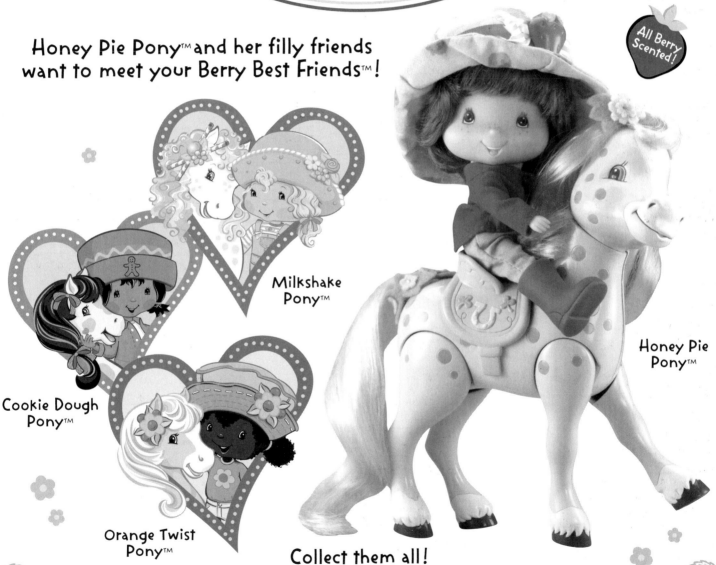

Honey Pie Pony™ and her filly friends want to meet your Berry Best Friends™!

All Berry Scented!

Milkshake Pony™

Cookie Dough Pony™

Orange Twist Pony™

Honey Pie Pony™

Collect them all!
Each sold separately

$6.99 US
($9.99 CAN)

Grow better with Strawberry Shortcake!

- Learn all about how plants grow—from seed to flower
- Plant your berry own berry patch
- Pick the prettiest flowers for your garden
- Bring out the butterflies by planting a butterfly garden
- Celebrate special days all year long by planting birthday trees

Packed with info about plants and how they grow, fun gardening projects, and a sweet story about Strawberry Shortcake's garden, this book is perfect for budding young gardeners!

GROSSET & DUNLAP

ISBN 0-448-43552-7

43552

UPC

0 70918 00699 9